TO: _____

From _____

A Mother's Gift

CHRIS SHEA

THOMAS NELSON
Since 1798

NASHVILLE   DALLAS   MEXICO CITY   RIO DE JANEIRO   BEIJING

Published in Nashville, Tennessee, by Thomas Nelson. Thomas Nelson is a registered trademark of Thomas Nelson, Inc.

Design by The DesignWorks Group and Robin Black, Blackbird Creative.

Thomas Nelson, Inc., titles may be purchased in bulk for educational, business, fund-raising, or sales promotional use. For information, please e-mail SpecialMarkets@ThomasNelson.com.

ISBN: 978-1-4041-8793-1

www.thomasnelson.com

Printed and bound in China

for my sister Susan Wong
and
my brother David Givens,
the best gifts my mother gave
me ...

Mothers give us many gifts...

Warm pajamas
made of flannel,

fuzzy little teddy bears,

squeaky
　yellow
　　rubber
　　　duckies

for bathtime in
the evening,

and ice cold

milk and

    sugar cookies

for after-school
delightful treats.

But the
best gift
mothers give
us

Is their
love,

a love

that only
moms
could give.

It warms
us up

in wintertime,

refreshes us

in
summer

and brightens up
the
darkest
night

when nightmares
come to call.

The love that mothers
give to us

makes boo-boos
feel
all better

and finds a way
to mend
our hearts

when they've
been badly
broken.

No one
else on
earth

can love
us like our
mothers,

not our kitty

or our doggy,

not our very best
friend

or our trusted,
worn stuffed toy,

because

mothers love us
with a love
that
never ends.

If we break
a dish or
spill the
milk

or forget to
feed the goldfish,

mothers love
us anyway;

that's a mother's
gift.

Mothers
show us
how
to count

on fingers
and on toes.

They sing to us
of
twinkling
stars

and rowing boats

and Mary and her lamb.

They read to us
from cherished
books

(and then pretend we're
reading too, when all we've
done is memorize the words
we've heard so often.)

Mothers are
the
Keepers

of our deepest
childhood
secrets,

our first
and
most important
teacher,

Hot!

kitchen table
artist,

Like this, Mommy?

dance instructor,

costume maker

and the one
who always shows us,
no matter how old
we grow,

the amazing things
a simple hug
can do.

Thank you
for being my
mother,

for the gifts
of guidance,
love,
and endless patience
you've poured into
my life.

Though many people
only read about the
heroes in
this world,

I've been blessed by
a wonderful gift:
my hero is my
mom!

I love you.